The Wedding Portrait

Innosanto Nagara

Author of *A is for Activist* and
My Night in the Planetarium

The story of a photograph and why
sometimes we break the rules

TRIANGLE
SQUARE
books for young readers

SEVEN STORIES 7

New York • Oakland • London

"Let your life be a counter-friction to stop the machine."

—Henry David Thoreau, *Civil Disobedience*

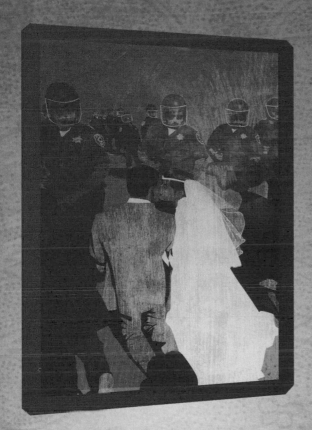

When kids visit our house, they often ask about a
particular photo that hangs on the wall. It's actually a
cutout from the newspaper, but we put it in a
frame and hung it up with the other family photos.

It's a wedding portrait: a picture of two people dressed up
for a wedding, kissing. Those two people are Mama and I
when we got married.

But as you can see, there is something different about this
wedding portrait!

But before I tell you about the portrait, I want to say something about breaking the rules.

We usually follow the rules. But sometimes, when you see something wrong—more wrong than breaking the rules, and by breaking the rules you could stop it—you may decide that you should break the rules.

You know about SEGREGATION, right? That was when in some parts of the United States there were laws against black people. Black families were not allowed to live in white neighborhoods. Black children had to go to separate schools and drink from separate water fountains. And when you got on the bus, if you were black, you had to sit in the back. Those were the rules—that was the law.

But those laws were racist. Those rules were wrong.

So some people decided to do something about it. Black activists would get on a bus and refuse to sit in the back. One of the first to do this was Claudette Colvin, who was just 15 years old. The bus driver yelled at her, "Move to the back!" But she ignored him. The driver called the police and the policemen yelled at her too, "Move to the back, or we'll arrest you!" She ignored them too.

The police arrested her.

But then other people came and sat in the front of the bus and refused to move. This happened over and over. Rosa Parks got on a bus and refused to move. The newspapers heard this was happening and came and took pictures. People from all over the country saw the pictures in the newspaper, and more came. Some marched. Some protested. Others got on buses and refused to move to the back.

And guess what? In the end, the laws were changed.

This is called CIVIL DISOBEDIENCE.

People have been using civil disobedience to fight for freedom for a long time. For instance, the British Empire colonized India for HUNDREDS of years. They stole their resources. They treated the people very badly. If anyone complained, they threw them in jail. And when people rebelled, the British used their army and guns to stop them.

This was not good.

So the people said, "Sorry, British Empire, but it's time for you to go home. And until you go, we won't be cooperating with you anymore." That playdate was over.

The British didn't want to go home, and tried to force the Indian people to keep following their rules. But the Indian people stuck to their promise. When the British told them they couldn't make their own clothes, they made their own clothes anyway. When the British tried to get them to pay taxes, they ignored them.

The British even tried to tell them they couldn't make their own salt from the sea! So thousands of people marched to the sea to make salt.

Some of the leaders were arrested. But others took their place and did it again. And again. And again. Over EIGHTY THOUSAND people were arrested for making salt.

They didn't win right away. But guess what? In the end, the British had to go home.

In Colombia, there is a nation of INDIGENOUS people who are called the U'wa. If you are indigenous to a place, that means you and your ancestors have been there for a long, long time. Thousands of years. Basically, forever.

The U'wa are also called the "Thinking People." Their homeland is known as *Kajka-Ika* or *Kera Chikara* and includes the headwaters of the Orinoco River. It is a beautiful place.

But their land is also a place where oil companies want to drill for oil.

The U'wa people knew that oil drilling only brings violence and environmental destruction. So they said, "No thank you." But the oil companies ignored them, and came anyway. So the U'wa people decided to go to the place where the company was going to drill for oil and set up a camp. They blocked the road into the camp to keep the oil company trucks from coming in. This is called a BLOCKADE.

People from all over the world heard about the blockade, and many went to the company's offices to protest along with the U'wa people. This is called SOLIDARITY. They also called for people to stop buying that company's oil, so that the oil company wouldn't make any money. This is called a BOYCOTT.

It took ten years. But guess what? In the end, the oil company went home.

NO A LA EXPLORACIÓN, NI
EXPLOTACIÓN EN EL
TERRITORIO ANCESTRAL UW

Another boycott was one led by
farmworkers in Immokalee, Florida.
These farmworkers are the people
who pick the tomatoes we eat. They
work really hard in the hot sun,
and are not paid very much. In fact,
some were being forced to work
for no pay at all! This was a case
of modern-day slavery.

So the farmworkers began to organize. They asked restaurant and supermarket owners to sign an agreement to only buy tomatoes from farms that treated their workers fairly.

But the owners said, "No way, we don't care about the farmworkers, we like our tomatoes cheap."

A lot of us don't have a lot of money, so we like our stuff cheap too, don't we? But think about it . . . if someone offered you a cheap tomato, but it was cheap because it was picked by a kid just like you who had to work all day for no pay and wasn't allowed to go home, would you buy it anyway?

I didn't think so. And the Immokalee workers didn't think so either. So they said, "Let's BOYCOTT those restaurants and supermarkets that don't care!"

food justice

BOYCOTT

They also held marches and rallies to let people know about the boycott. At one point they marched almost 250 miles! All the way to Orlando. People across the country stopped going to those restaurants and supermarkets.

And guess what? In the end, the restaurants and supermarkets decided they had better care.

There are many different kinds of civil disobedience and direct action. There is the Sit-In, the Lockdown, the Sick-Out, the Slow-Down, the Work-to-Rule, the Strike, the Boycott, and the Blockade. You can be a War-Tax Resister, a Conscientious Objector, a Banner Dropper, a Tree Sitter, a Hunger Striker, a Plowsharer, or a Whistle-Blower.

And people are always finding new and creative forms of civil disobedience.

Black Lives Matter activists wanted to get rid of the Confederate Flag. That's the flag of the people who wanted to keep slavery during the U.S. Civil War. They lost the war, and slavery was banned. But even though the flag is a symbol of racism, some state governments were still flying it.

So Bree Newsome and her friend James Tyson decided to do something about it. They got up really early one morning, and went to the government building where the flag was flying. While her friends helped as look-outs, Bree climbed up the flagpole and took down the flag. This is called DIRECT ACTION.

The police came and made her come down. Then they arrested her. But by then lots of people had seen Bree on TV taking down the flag. They joined in demanding that the flag come down.

And guess what? Less than a month later, the flag was taken down for good.

Now. I'll bet all this is giving you some ideas, isn't it? Do you think some of the things that you do when you're not following the rules should be considered civil disobedience? Do you think hiding under the bed to avoid taking a bath is a kind of sit-in? Is refusing to eat your dinner a kind of boycott?

Maybe. (Maybe not.)

But I was supposed to be telling you about that wedding portrait.

It all started because Mama and I don't like NUCLEAR WEAPONS. Nuclear weapons are huge, terrible, expensive bombs that are so deadly they can blow up a whole city. And after the bomb blows up the city, it leaves poisonous RADIATION everywhere that makes people sick.

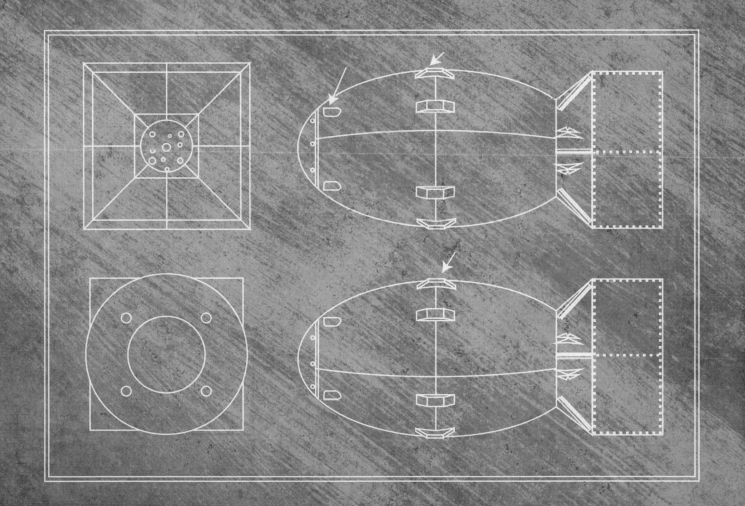

Nuclear bombs had only been used in one war. Long before you were born, during World War II, the United States dropped two nuclear bombs: one on the city of Hiroshima and one on the city of Nagasaki, in Japan. These were cities full of regular people, and many, many people died. And because of radiation, even more people got sick.

Then other countries wanted to have nuclear bombs. They figured if their neighbors had one and they didn't, and they got into a war, they would lose. This became known as the ARMS RACE. Countries were racing to see who could make the most nuclear weapons the fastest.

But regular people like us were against this arms race. We understood that if everyone had big deadly bombs, and a war did start, then everyone would get bombed. And it would be terrible. And sad. And there would be no happy ending.

It's like if you hit someone because you don't like what they said, and they hit you back harder, and you then hit them back even harder . . . nothing gets better and everyone gets hurt.

And when you do it with nuclear bombs, everyone dies. Who wants that?

So people protested against nuclear bombs. Anti-nuclear activists would go to places where the military was testing its new weapons, and try to get in the way so they couldn't do their tests. This is called a SIT-IN. Native American communities, like the Western Shoshone people, led these protests because it was their land that was being poisoned by the radiation from these nuclear tests.

Many others came in solidarity.

Meanwhile Mama and I had decided that we wanted to get married. We had been living together for many years, we were in love, and we wanted our families and friends to join us in celebrating our love. We also thought it was important that we used the occasion to celebrate the values that brought us together. We had first met on a bus going to a protest. So we decided to take our wedding to a protest!

People get all dressed up to look nice for a wedding. I was in a suit. And Mama was in a beautiful white wedding dress. All our friends who were part of the ceremony were also dressed nicely. Then we all marched together to a lab where the government made new weapons and we stood in front of the gates.

We were blocking the gates, so the guards came and told us we had to move.

Instead, we kneeled down. And just like in a regular wedding, we kissed, and everyone in the audience clapped. Even some of the guards had to smile.

They still wanted us to stop blocking the gates though, so they gave us a final warning, "If you don't move right away, we will arrest you!"

Do you think we moved?

No. We refused to move.
And they arrested us.

About 100 people
refused to move that day.

We had to sit in the sun
all afternoon. It was like
a super long time-out.
Mama's wedding dress
was all dusty and dirty.

But a reporter took a photo of us and published it in the newspaper. Lots of people read the newspaper and learned about what the government was doing.

Our friends thought that was the best wedding photo ever, so as a gift, they framed it and we hung it on our wall.

And guess what?

Wedding Party Arrested at Anti-Nuclear Protest

That is the story of the wedding portrait.

Epilogue

Many stones can form an arch,
Singly none, singly none.

(from the preamble to the constitution of the United Mine Workers of America)

That one photo did not get rid of the nuclear weapons problem. But it did help more people learn about what was going on, and those people came out and protested too, and some nuclear testing has been banned. But there are still a lot of nuclear weapons. And there are still laws that are racist. And there are still oil companies that are trying to drill for oil and build pipelines on indigenous peoples' lands. These are problems that we continue to work on today.

My story is about taking action. But it is also about working together. Things can only get better when people work together. One person can make a difference, but it's not usually just one thing that one person does that changes things. Not everyone can break the rules and risk getting arrested. Not everyone who takes action gets noticed. The stories I've told you here are not the whole story. The whole story would take books and books and books to tell. The whole story would tell you about the people who did civil disobedience, but it would also tell you about the people who wrote letters, marched, knocked on doors, taught others, created art and music, and did a million other things toward change. Also, making the world a better place isn't just about stopping the stuff we don't like. It's also about showing better ways of doing things. It's going to take all of us.

■ ■ ■

For more information on the ongoing struggles mentioned in this book, and how to support them and get involved, visit:

AisforActivist.com

**Dedicated to Arief Romero
& his mama, Kristi**

Special thanks to Sacha, Jupi, Jaiah, Marcos, Lucia,
Arief, Amado, Mayari, Mico, Joaquin, Kavi, Silar, Ila,
Theo, Emma, William, Sam, Tossan, Aiko, Mabel, Miles,
Ena, Anna, Eva, Helen, Miguel, Analu, Asher, Dezi, Kaya,
Camilo, Paloma, Sadie, Thea, Bridger, Harldur, Hugo,
Thomas, Andie, the Berkwood Hedge kids, the Abundant
Beginnings kids, and everyone else who test-drove this
book and shared your insights and critical feedback.

Text and artwork © 2017 by Innosanto Nagara

A Triangle Square Books for Young Readers edition, published by
Seven Stories Press

Seven Stories Press
140 Watts Street
New York, NY 10013
www.sevenstories.com

Library of Congress Cataloging-in-Publication Data

Names: Nagara, Innosanto, author.
Title: The wedding portrait / Innosanto Nagara.
Description: A Seven Stories Press first edition. I New York : Seven
Stories
   Press, [2017] I Audience: Age 6-9. I Audience: Grade K to grade 3.
Identifiers: LCCN 2017003752 (print) I LCCN 2017026766 (ebook) I
ISBN 9781609808037 (E-book) I ISBN 9781609808020 (hardcover)
Subjects: LCSH: Civil disobedience--Juvenile literature.
Classification: LCC JC328.3 (ebook) I LCC JC328.3 .N336 2017
(print) I DDC
   303.6/1--dc23
LC record available at https://lccn.loc.gov/2017003752

Printed in China.